YOU KNOW YOU'RE IN
CHARLOTTE IF...

YOU KNOW YOU'RE IN CHARLOTTE IF...

by
Margaret G. Bigger

Illustrated by Loyd Dillon

With a Local Sports History Quiz by Jack Wood

ABB

A. Borough Books

ISBN 1-893597-03-2

Library of Congress Control Number 00-133196

Printed in the United States of America

Cover design by Loyd Dillon
Illustrations by Loyd Dillon

ABB

A. Borough Books
P.O. Box 15391
Charlotte NC 28211

PREFACE

Oops, we made a mistake when we wrote *You Can Tell You're a Charlottean If...*. Our last line was "You're considered a native if...you've been here a full year." Some people born here sniffed their offense. Frankly, we thought that superior "born here" attitude had gone out with the white-gloves-and-hats-downtown era. If we could do it over again, we'd put quotation marks around the word "native." Even so, the REAL natives *did* seem to like our book.

Others glanced at the title, "That's not for me; I'm not a Charlottean."

"How long have you lived here?" my co-editor Betsy Webb or I would ask.

"Twenty years."

The best response to "You're considered a native if you've been here a full year," however, was: "And that only includes 50% of us!"

Perhaps that's why a new line, suggested by more than one person, is "You're in Charlotte if you're not from 'round here."

Now, we aim to be even more inclusive. We not only recognize the long-timers but the 50% who have just dropped in and are trying to get accustomed to our ways. Not only that, we have recorded the views of some outsiders as well.

This time we include everyone who happens to be here at the moment—and those who wish they could be.

ACKNOWLEDGMENTS

Although many of the lines are from former contributors, we appreciate the help of *The Leader* and Borders Books & Music in Morrocroft Village, who encouraged more people to give us their views about Charlotte.

Denise Dory, newscaster for WTVI and WBTV, former broadcaster Cameron Garrison on WBT and longtime radio personality Henry Boggan, who was substituting on WMNX ("Mix 106") one day, solicited lines from their viewers and listeners. *Charlotte* magazine and *The Charlotte Observer's* Business Monday also suggested numerous ideas.

A hearty thanks to them and to all the current—and former—Charlotte residents who supplied the thoughts that made us chuckle or react with a "I didn't know that!" "Oh, wow!" or "Say WHAT?" See the List of Contributors for their names. The most outstanding is Jack Wood, who shared his nearly 90 years of sports knowledge, to give us a bonus Local Sports History Quiz.

Please know that we are grateful as well to those of you who said something "in passing" which materialized later on paper.

LIST OF CONTRIBUTORS

Bet Ancrum	Joy Christenbury	Jo Anne Ellis
Sandra Banks	Ann Sawyer Cleland	Sue Elrod
Chuck Barnes	Debbie Cline	Julie Farhi
Anilee Lewis Bateman	Phil Clutts	Sandy Fisher
Randy Bigger	Robert Covington	Chris Folk
Yvette Bissent	Mike Cozza	Ann Wright Galant
Randall Bloomquist	Mitchell B. Craig	Bill Golden
Henry Boggan	Anne Way Crawford	Cissy Gottlieb
Donna Brim	John Curry	Glenn T. Griffin
Gwen Brown	Michael Daisley	John Hancock
Jill Butterworth	John F. Darracott	Robert Harrell
Rob Carpenter	Loyd Dillon	Granville Hearn
Phil Casper	Scott Dodd	Robert Hefner
Tracy Casper	M. Scott Douglas	Janet Hince
Bonnie Chavda	Marian Duffee	Karen Hollingsworth

LIST OF CONTRIBUTORS

Memory Honeycutt
Mary Huffman
Robert R. Jewell
Jimmy Kilgo
Bill Kumerow
Bob Kumerow
Margie Cowell Lee
Doug Little
Gray Little
Laura Lyerly
Robin Marcnovic
James E. Martin, Jr.
Katherine McAdams
Cathy McGill
Loonis McGlohon

Ryan McGuire
Pamela Minerd
Tucker Mitchell
Gregory Lee Moore
Tracy Newsome
Karen Nolan
Durward Owen
D'Arlene Pound
Amelia Powell
John Rasberry
F. Marion Redd
Joe Robinson
Leonard Robinson
Millie Robinson
Robbie Robinson

Bruce Rosenberg
Philip Shore, Jr.
Gwen Spann
Lee Stiles
John Syme
Betty Barrett Temple
Pete Temple
Charles H. Thomas
Paul M. Visser
Ileene Silvers Wallace
Harry C. Washington
Betsy Webb
Nancy Whitehurst
Jack Wood
Linda Walker Wooten

CONTENTS

YOU KNOW YOU'RE IN CHARLOTTE IF...

Even if you're just passing through:

You're stuck in traffic.

Or you're caught in "Charlotte's web" from driving in circles and criss-crossing your own path.

The street changed names at the last intersection.

You get a souvenir photo of your car's rear end and license tag, compliments of the city.*

* To obtain this souvenir, you must run a red light. By the way, it's not free. Oh, and don't try anything crazy. Those cameras are in bullet-proof boxes.

YOU KNOW YOU'RE IN CHARLOTTE IF...

Every few blocks, there's a large drug store on a corner.

Green road signs say "downtown," but blue signs on light poles call it "uptown."

Cell phone towers are outgrowing—and outnumbering—trees.

Orange and white striped barrels outnumber pedestrians.

While waiting for traffic, you have time to read bumper stickers.

Main Street is not downtown. (It runs between Baldwin and Baxter Streets.)

YOU KNOW YOU'RE IN CHARLOTTE IF...

At night, you see a big jukebox with green neon and the Taj McColl dominating the skyline.

In the daytime, you can watch Ed Crutchfield and Hugh McColl competing for the biggest erection yet.

New housing lots are so small that you really can pass a cup of sugar from your window to your neighbor's.

Seasons change every three to five days in the wintertime.

Casual Friday is fast becoming Casual Everyday/Slovenly Friday.

YOU KNOW YOU'RE IN CHARLOTTE IF...

Someone invites you to join him at "the club." (Which? Too many to count!)

The city magazine that touts the greatness of Charlotte then tells you where to go to get away.

The local TV news tries to give "news you can use," but it's still a body count.

You hear a radio station* which broadcasts a 6-minute tape over and over and...

A 6th level walkway takes you to the 2nd level of a major building.**

* WCSR has a two-mile range around Ballantyne.
** From the Bank of America parking garage to Founders Hall.

YOU KNOW YOU'RE IN CHARLOTTE IF...

Salespeople are actually polite and say "thank you."

On the other hand, other people are holding cell phones to their ears while:
- making a left turn toward some wide-eyed drivers.
- walking through a crowd and frowning at their noise.
- sitting at a bar amidst a host of eavesdroppers.
- standing in a fast food line, checking fellow construction workers' orders.
- munching on dinner and conversing with business associates.
- hunching over grocery produce, asking what else she wants him to buy.
- lunching alone, but not all alone, for his other pocket is ringing.

In 1998, Charlotte ranked 2nd in cell phone ownership. 54% use them.

Health nuts are jogging among the dead (in cemeteries) or running in the streets, defying drivers and death, too.

YOU KNOW YOU'RE IN CHARLOTTE IF...

You have numerous choices of airline flights but will spend all your vacation money getting there.

You can choose from many fine restaurants now, but, if you're not on an expense account, you could spend a day's (even a week's) pay on a meal.

Residents seem to be "in another world." Perhaps it's because we have more movie screens per capita here.

The buildings that appear to be historic are probably new, designed to look old.

Locals don't have "clay feet," just clay on the shoes. (You will, too!)

YOU KNOW YOU'RE IN CHARLOTTE IF...

Fan City

You've been buzzed by the biggest insect you've ever seen: Air Hindenbug.

You have to duck for Chuck-a-Pucks and burritos at Checkers games.

You see residents LEAVING during Speed Week.

At an NFL game, Ric Flair gets more attention than the team.

You've heard that the Sunset Club and Belle Acres Country Club have something to do with sports. (If you've only "heard," you're probably not "eligible.")

YOU KNOW YOU'RE IN CHARLOTTE IF...

You join locals imitating Romans reveling in the stadium while panthers try to devour lions, bears, jaguars, falcons, eagles and ravens.

The best-dressed sports fans are at the Johnson C. Smith Queen City Classic.

The city's AAA baseball league stadium and headquarters are in another state. (The Charlotte Knights are at Fort Mill, SC.)

The principal owner of the local NBA team not only doesn't call Charlotte home—he doesn't even live in the Carolinas!

"Mason" brings to mind "jarring jams" and "in the can."

YOU KNOW YOU'RE IN CHARLOTTE IF...

Fine Place to Dine

At least 90% of the local eating establishments serve french fries. Ketchup, too!

The grits are *good!*

You can count on getting warm bread, but only at locally-owned eateries.

Someone leaving the restaurant in front of you is picking his teeth.

Lunchtime begins a little after 11 a.m. Its duration depends on how important a client you are.

YOU KNOW YOU'RE IN CHARLOTTE IF...

Chances are pretty good that:

You get lost at least once a week.

You've never sampled much of the delicious ethnic foods available here.

You've never noticed the local historic sites. (Only a few are still standing.)

Most of the people around you are not Charlotte natives, nor even long-time residents. In a few years, they may not even be from this country.

You're probably not from 'round here.

YOU'RE A "NATIVE" IF...

Remember, this means you've been here a full year — or more!

Your kids' clothes have permanent red-clay stains.

You've got ketchup on the table, a basketball goal in the yard and a pickup (or an "assault vehicle") in your garage.

In this mostly sweater-weather town, you have a sweater for every occasion, even the 4th of July.

You really do appreciate the beautiful trees in this "City of Trees" and hate to see bulldozers knocking them down like bowling pins.

YOU'RE A "NATIVE" IF...

You've wondered how Queen Charlotte in the Mint Museum portrait, the statue in front of the Trade Center and the sculpture at the airport could possibly be the same person.

If you work in the central city, the property owner there will likely have "bank" or "Duke" in its name.

If you're successful in business locally, you have learned the importance of the 4 Cs: you must join the Chamber of Commerce, a charity, a club and last, but certainly not least, a church.

You know the difference between CPCC and CCCP.*

* Central Piedmont Community College and Charlotte Center City Partners

YOU'RE A "NATIVE" IF...

At least one of your children goes to a one-room schoolhouse (mobile classroom).

Your teen's prom preparations at SouthPark cost more than your wedding.

Even if you dress like a redneck, you'd NEVER belch in public after a meal.

In this the ketchup capital of the world, you'll NEVER support the green version.

You've heard why the trolley goes only to a parking lot on the edge of the center city and never gets to the 7th Street Station.**

* Because, while trolley preservationists were planning the route, transportation officials ordered the railroad bridge over Stonewall Street demolished.

YOU'RE A "NATIVE" IF...

You've watched people park in the handicapped lot and then walk the three-building maze of the Southern Christmas Show.

You chuckled when the Millennium Blowout planners waffled cutely with the city core's identity by calling the event the "Uptown Downtown Countdown."

You thought it amusing that the Mecklenburg Alcoholic Beverage Control board chairman gave himself a 40th birthday bash at a saloon (called "Belly Ache-ers").

You're acquainted with the Charlotte celebrities Horace and Doris, Sagacious McThrift and Gus.*

* Griffin Motor Co. puppets, Scottish Bank's symbolic leader, Gus the Talking (school safety) Bus

YOU'RE A "NATIVE" IF...

When you see a snowflake or hear a hurricane warning, you rush out to buy stuff that will rot in three days (except the beer).

You declare your independence by flying your American flag or mowing your lawn despite the homeowners' association rules.

You've READ Independence Boulevard ("the arts thang").

Even if you're a conservative transplant, you think the "liberal rag" makes sense most of the time.

When people make fun of our "world class city," you admit it isn't—YET.

YOU'RE A "NATIVE" IF...

Dizzy Drivin'

Mass transit, for now, is packing all the kids in your gas-guzzling van.

A yield sign is a personal challenge.

Stop signs with white borders seem to be optional.

You assume that using your blinkers alerts other drivers as to what they're not going to let you do.

You feel naked without a cell phone on I-77.

YOU'RE A "NATIVE" IF...

You've given every orange barrel on Providence Road a pet name.

You can get from one side of town to the other without getting on Highway 74.

You're still confused by all the Queens and Sharon Roads. (14 have Queen or Queens in the name; 17 have a Sharon name.)

But, you can navigate Queens Road, Queens Road West and Queens Road East without making a U-turn.

If you're under 40, you speed over speed bumps; if you're over 60, you creep over them.

29

YOU'RE A "NATIVE" IF...

To you, 10 cars in a row is gridlock traffic.

You keep a book in your car to read at red lights.

You speed going to church.

It's a racing game to see if yours can be the second or third car to scoot under a red light.

You trust your car to a repair shop run by a well-dressed lady in diamonds and pearls.*

* Norris Auto Service

YOU'RE A "NATIVE" IF...

Arts & Entertainment

Until their new building is completed, you don't want too many others to find out that the "best Broadway for the buck" is CPCC's Summer Theatre.

You can't wait until *Art for a Steal*, the Loonis McGlohon/Mark DeCastrique musical about Gastonia's wacky Loomis Fargo heist, is a hit!

You gawk at the velvet dog hangings at Pat's Time Out for One More Tavern.

You know what Gunk, Liquid Wrench & Solder Seal has to do with art.*

* The Blumenthal Performing Arts Center is named for the parent company's founder

YOU'RE A "NATIVE" IF...

You think the old Mint Museum and the new NoDa galleries are fine, but your favorite murals are in the Dunhill Hotel garage.

You like to visit Great Aunt Stella, but you're still waiting to meet Great Uncle What's-His-Name.

You worry when your spouse says, "Honey, I'm going to..."
- "Mother's" - a billiard parlor
- "The Office" - a lounge
- "The Old Stompin' Ground" - a tavern
- "Just Because" - a sports bar and lingerie lounge

Depending on your age, you're dancing again at Swing 1000 (big band), Coyote Joe's (country), Mythos (techno & disco), or at a "secret" rave gathering spot.

YOU'RE A "NATIVE" IF...

You have just as much fun as the preschoolers shooting water guns in the Kid's Place at Discovery Place.

If you're a part of Corporate Charlotte, you've probably donned camouflage, picked up a gun and shot some other "hot shots" with paintballs.

If you're not, you probably picked up plenty of guns at the NRA's national convention or your favorite supplier. You even carry one in your pickup, in case a rhino charges your Ram.

If you're really trendy, you've raced fellow execs in a "boy toy" cart, then "braked" for a business conference at Victory Lane.

YOU'RE A "NATIVE" IF...

Eager Eaters

You know to order the sesame chicken at Shun Lee Palace, buffet at Tsing Tao, satay at the Thai House, lettuce wraps at P.F. Chang's China Bistro and to watch out for the "medium hot" sauce at India Palace.

You enjoy the yams, cornbread and fried chicken at the Coffee Cup, but you miss the prime rib and desserts at Windows on Trade, a great place to see and be seen.

You see the irony in the Hard Times Cafe location at Piper Glen.

Your favorite pizza restaurant misspells your order. (Wolfman's calls a bacon, spinach and tomato pizza a BLT.)

YOU'RE A "NATIVE" IF...

You've figured out which fast food places give IQ tests to hire the ones who fail.

You get your "hot dog fix" on weekdays at Green's Lunch. (You're a reeeal native if you go to Green's on Saturdays.)

If you're a 4th Warder, you're not afraid to order the "what it is" at Al Mike's.

If you wear shorts year 'round, Jack Mackeral's is your Margaritaville.

Although CJ's claims to be Charlotte's "best kept secret" (maybe because it's not in the phone book), you know that, for great food, good music and fast seating, go to...(Shhhhhh! It's a secret!)

YOU'RE A "NATIVE" IF...

You've discovered that Zydeco's delicious seafood comes from the Marais kitchen at about half the price.

You got your best black history lesson from the walls of Mert's Heart and Soul.

You know that Eddie's Place is really Danny's, Too.

You're scratching your head: If Sullivan's Steakhouse is named for America's heavyweight champion in the 1880s, how come the decor is 1940's style?

Even with all the fine specialty restaurants in town, you know to go to Pineville to take your best friend to a canine cafe (Barbara's).

YOU'RE A "NATIVE" IF...

Fanatic Fans, Who Us?

You don't mind being black and blue, especially on Fridays. (Sundays, too!)

You've wondered why the Sting don't have macho male cheerleaders known as the Horny Hornets. (Well, if the Hornets can have HoneyBEES, why can't the Sting team have Hornets?)

You feel cheated that Michael Jordan is leading the Washington Wizards instead of the Hornets.

You find it surprising that Charlotte seems to be changing from a "basketball town" to a "football/baseball city."

YOU'RE A "NATIVE" IF...

You think the jersey designed by the young teenage fan is better looking than the Checkers' official one.

You recognize the appropriateness of naming our next pro team the Charlotte Bankers, which would have pinstripe blue uniforms and a mascot dressed like Monopoly's Uncle Pennybags.

You've seen the kid reported to have had the biggest feet in a Charlotte-area day care center (ex-Hornet Larry Johnson's son).

You have purchased a PSL that guarantees not a seat but a space for generations to come. (That is, if the "social event of the year"* is important to you.)

* The Queen's Cup Steeplechase

YOU'RE A "NATIVE" IF...

You've been taking binoculars to the Hive—to inspect the Honeybees.

You know that the Charlotte Motor Speedway (now Lowe's) never was in the city of Charlotte.

You saw the humor in City Council having to decide between what WBTV's Mike Cozza calls "fish or foul" (an aquarium vs. a new basketball arena).

You'd consider the idea of a new aquarium/arena complex, but it's sure to get the nickname "Fish Bowl."

You still have a huge hole in your heart for "Mighty Mouse" Mugsy.

YOU'RE A REEEAL NATIVE IF...

Born here? Sure. Been around since at least 1965 and drank your first Cheerwine and Bud here? You can relate to this, too.

You frequently get lost because you don't own an up-to-date map (wouldn't use it, if you had one).

You pick up a visitor's guide and see ads for places you've never heard of and wouldn't dream of going to.

If you're Scots-Irish, you think bagpipes are melodious.*

* Didn't anyone inform you that your ancestors' armies used bagpipes to terrify the enemy?

YOU'RE A REEEAL NATIVE IF...

Your Southern accent sounds nothing like the Hollywood version.

You thought Dilworth was on the other side of the tracks.

Your children still say "Yes ma'm" and "No sir."

You used to assume *out loud* that all poor drivers were from South Carolina.

At some time, you've owned a car "guaranteed by Louis F. Harrelson."

You left town, but came back.

YOU'RE A REEEAL NATIVE IF...

You and your friends went "trick or treating" safely with NO PARENTS.

You couldn't understand why your dad wanted to take you to buy Buster Brown shoes at Thompson's Bootery & Bloomery.*

The Monday night wrestling matches you attended at Park Center were G-rated (or at least I-rated for "innocent").

You really miss the HIGH SCHOOL Queen City Classic.**

* They sold sexy lingerie, too, sometimes on live models.

** The final football game between West Charlotte and Second Ward was played in 1969.

YOU'RE A REEEAL NATIVE IF...

Tasty Treats

You count Spam as one of the basic food groups.

You don't drink root beer with pizza (Cheerwine, maybe, but never root beer).

You think paprika is spicy.

You've been slurping milk shakes from Mr. K's since you were a kid, and now you're taking your children.

You bought groceries from the Siamese twins at Park-N-Shop on Wilkinson.

YOU'RE A REEEAL NATIVE IF...

It never bothered you that Ivey's Tulip Terrace was not a terrace and had fake tulips.

You knew by sniffing when Jack's Cookie Company was baking coconut cookies.

You concede that the old standby Beef 'N Bottle may look like a joint, but you'll match their steaks to those "high-falutin,' high-dollar" steak places.

You recall when so many locals were insistent beef-eaters that the town's one unique restaurant (The Luau) had to add an American steak menu.

You're amazed that Spoon's on Hawthorne no longer makes Spoon's Ice Cream.

YOU'RE A REEEAL NATIVE IF...

History & Geography

You know enough about Charlotte history to realize it's been a "suck up" city ever since leaders named it for the Queen of England to flatter the king.

You actually know what Meck Dec is and where Meck Neck was.*

You're aware that the most influential secret document whose historical authenticity is still in dispute is not the Meck Dec but an annual report written by Charlotte's "movers and shakers" known as "The View From Way Up Here."

* Mecklenburg's declaration of independence from England, written more than a year before the national one (May 20, 1775). / After Lake Norman was formed, a neck of Mecklenburg County land was cut off from county services until it became part of Iredell County in 1998.

YOU'RE A REEEAL NATIVE IF...

You've hunted for an entrance to a gold mine (perhaps even skipped recess at Barringer School to find one).

Though not related to Hezekiah Alexander, you've visited his home at least once.

You can properly pronounce the names of former owners of historic homes, such as the Thies and Gluyas families.**

** Thies rhymes with geese; Gluyas rhymes with Lewis

Oh, yes...

You still love Charlotte, no matter what.

YOU'VE BEEN AROUND A REEEAL LONG TIME IF...

This applies to anyone who has been around since before 1965, particularly if you grew up here.

Your current friends are kids from your grammar school.

You've been meeting your friends in "Harry & Bryant's Waiting Room," better known as The Barclay Cafeteria.

You never go to the "South Boulevard Country Club" (The Cupboard) between 11:30 a.m. and 2 p.m.

You can drink Blenheim's ginger ale without it bringing tears to your eyes.

YOU'VE BEEN AROUND A REEEAL LONG TIME IF...

Your only TV appearances were in Uncle Bill's Clubhouse, on Captain Phil's show or with everybody's favorite cowboy, Fred Kirby.

You saw Minnie Pearl, Eddie Arnold and Red Foley at the Broadway Theater.

You knew that WSOC-TV's Joey the Clown was really Brooks Lindsay.

You watched WBTV's cooking star Betty Feezor have trouble grocery shopping because her fans got in the way.

You ever tried some of those Crazy Water Crystals that WBT's Grady Cole and the Briarhoppers used to talk about. (A so-called cure-all discredited in 1940.)

YOU'VE BEEN AROUND A REEEAL LONG TIME IF...

You were aware that city decisions not made at City Council or the City Club were generated at the Hoot Mon, including the support of Fred Alexander, the first African-American city councilman.

You recall when the city tried to close Wallace's Delicatessen for selling sour cream.

You know that Park Road was named for Latta Park, not Park Road Park.

You were shocked by the cartoon of His Honor and Her Honor in bed together, even though they were married.*

*It appeared after the wedding of Mayor John Belk and Judge Claudia Watkins in 1971.

YOU'VE BEEN AROUND A REEEAL LONG TIME IF...

You knew better than to try to buy a sherry glass, card tables, bridge items—or even the color burgundy—at Ivey's.

You sat down to shop at Montaldo's; the saleslady brought clothes to inspect.

You never ever, ever, ever, ever called a streetcar a trolley!

You lined up to buy gas on Saturday evenings, because filling stations were not open on Sundays.

One of your parents or grandparents went to Alexander Graham *High* School.*

* A high school from the spring of '20-'23, it became a junior high when Central opened.

YOU'VE BEEN AROUND A REEEAL LONG TIME IF...

You were around when the most exclusive (based on percentage of population) neighborhood was (brace yourself, Myers Parkers) Washington Heights.

You wondered how the area known for coal clouds got its name: Blue Heaven.

You followed the aroma to Merita Bakery on West Trade, where you peered through the windows to watch loaves go down rollers.

You ate at Anderson's Restaurant when it was in a streetcar.

You could lunch at the S & W Cafeteria downtown for 52¢, and that included strawberry shortcake.

YOU'VE BEEN AROUND A REEEAL LONG TIME IF...

High School Years

You got your first kiss on the ferris wheel at Airport Park.

You smooched in the balcony of the Imperial or the Carolina Theater.

A typical date was a movie in a theater and a hamburger and milkshake at Honey's Drive-In; a cheap date was when guys piled into the trunk of a car a block away from the drive-in theater so they only had to pay the girls' admission.

Your friends drove to Fort Mill to buy a gallon of liquor each, which they sold in Charlotte to get date money. (Of course, you never did that!)

YOU'VE BEEN AROUND A REEEAL LONG TIME IF...

You spent many a Friday night at Memorial Stadium watching local rivals break bones and knock teeth out at football games.

You and your friends took off for Myrtle Beach on Mother's Day weekend (with chaperones, of course), leaving Mom at home.

You took advantage of the fact that the back parking lot of Harrell's Barbecue had no lights.

Depending on your age, you listened to d.j. idol Jimmy Kilgo on WIST radio, went to see him at Playland Park (now the site of the Paper Doll Lounge) or danced at the popular Kilgo's Canteen on WSOC-TV.

YOU'VE BEEN AROUND A REEEAL LONG TIME IF...

You got out of school one afternoon every fall to go to the county fair, but you rarely went to the fair.

You square danced in the summer and skated in the winter on Freedom Park's round skating rink.

If you're a male, you enjoyed the "Central Smokers," fund-raiser boxing matches with only Central High boxers in the early '50s. If you're female, you delighted in watching the Queens College girls dance around the May pole every May Day.

Oh and...

When asked if you've lived in Charlotte all your life, you respond, "Not yet!"

YOU'RE A NEWCOMER IF...

Referring to the 50% who've been here less than a year:

You're more likely to meet someone from your own hometown than a REEEAL Charlotte native.

You haven't a *clue* what "Tuesday week" means.

You snicker while the rest of us try to drive in snow.

You try to take the Independence exit off I-77. (Okay, there *should* be one.)

You brought road rage with you. (Sorry, we didn't have it 5 years ago.)

YOU'RE A NEWCOMER IF...

You wonder why it took people of normal intelligence 6 years to get out of South Mecklenburg High.*

Until recently, you thought Salisbury was a steak. Now, it's a real stretch to believe that "Smallsbury" was ever bigger than Charlotte.

You were stunned when your boss expected you to give to certain charities, then checked to see if you complied—and now assumes you will do volunteer work.

You hang out at NoDa.**

* In the early '60s, until Quail Hollow Junior High was built, South had grades 7-12.

** Long-timers' clue: the cluster of art galleries and eateries on North Davidson

OUTSIDERS' OBSERVATIONS

How do others view Charlotte and Charlotteans? Well, we've come a long way in the Charleston-Charlotte-Charlottesville confusion—or have we?

* Although he didn't refer to Charlotte, Virginia, Michael Feldman on the "Whaddya Know" show spoke of Charlottesville, N.C.

* Some D.C. residents are sure we're in South Carolina.

* A former D.C. resident notes that it doesn't take long to figure out that the Bank of America and First Union are to this city what the federal government is to Washington.

* Many people outside of Virginia assume this is the hometown of Thomas Jefferson.

OUTSIDERS' OBSERVATIONS

* TV's Jeopardy! players couldn't name the hometown of the Carolina Panthers.

* A Wisconsin geographer coming here for a convention told a Charlotte colleague that he was looking forward to a tour of the harbor.

* A congressman from Idaho praised Charlotte and its mayor Joe Riley (Charleston's esteemed mayor).

* The *Wall Street Journal* wrote about the Mint Museum of Craft + Design in Charleston.

* Seimens headquarters sent *The Charlotte Observer* a list of the work force in their Westinghouse Power Corp. Plant in Charlotte, South Carolina.

* Wherever they're from, when they read about us, they call us charlatans.

OUTSIDERS' OBSERVATIONS

Now, "Charlotte USA" (including multiple counties, even Chester in South Carolina) is supposed to solve the CH problem. Anyone tried to mail a letter to "Charlotte USA"? Meanwhile, others have stated more interesting "facts" about this city:

* San Franciscans imagine NASCAR fans sitting around gnawing on pickled pigs feet. (They obviously haven't dined in the Speedway Club.)

* The *Washington Post* reported that Charlotte is a nice place to live, but you wouldn't want to visit. (Visit, please! Don't plan to stay!)

* Big-city slickers say "you'll grow old waiting for a taxi." (Try a shuttle.)

* A Harper's Ferry, West Virginia tourist is still laughing about the dull time he had in the "town" he calls "dead." (New York City Harper's Ferry is NOT. What do they have that we don't?)

CHARLOTTE CELEBRITIES

James Bond - frames houses
Kit Carson - drives for a parcel service
Vincent Foster - dispatcher, trucking company
George Hamilton - serves as a minister
Herbert Hoover - dentist
Andrew Jackson - electrician
Stonewall Jackson - grocery store manager
Van Johnson - mortgage company loan officer
John F. Kennedy - engineering manager
M. L. King - dispatcher for a power company
Michele Lee - client relations, website designer
James Madison - technician
Rex Morgan - attorney
Philip Morris - develops software solutions
Paul Newman - retired
Tony Randall - fixes transmissions

Donna Reed - designs African-American crafts
Randolph Scott - commercial construction management
Gene Simmons - car salesman
Elizabeth Taylor - retired
George Wallace - engineer

Some "Multiple Personalities" around here:

Henry Ford, Ben Franklin, James Garner, Jesse Helms, Robin Hood, John Paul Jones, Joseph Kennedy, Glenn Miller, General Washington, George Washington - 2 of each; **James Dean, Roy Rogers, Robert Stack** - 3; **Robert Kennedy, James Mason** - 4; **Jennifer Jones** - 5; **Gary Cooper** - 6; **James Stewart** - 11; **John Adams** - 14; **James Taylor** - 20, **James Brown** - 40

CUTE & CLEVER LICENSE PLATES

Just by checking out license plates in the area, you can learn a lot about Charlotteans—they're clever, yes, but more...

No doubt! We're in the Bible Belt.

2NDCOMIN	GODIS4US
BELEVGOD	GODISGR8
PRAIS GOD	GODSTRUE
THNKUGOD	G'SUSAVES
W/ANGELS	JESUS SVS
IAMBLESD	2JOHN1-3
BLESS U	GENESIS7
4HIMSING	J LOVES U
4 HYMN	WE LUV JC

Or ARE we?

TALKDRTY
NOHOPE4U
ETERNITY?
WHOCARES
WUT-EVRR
NEXTLIFE
GTERGRIP
GMEABRAK
HECKYEAH

Beer Belt, too!

BEERMAN
MUGZHLDR
THSBDZ4U
THIRSTY

A sophisticated city, huh?

SOOOI	FRUTCAKE
LITL MULE	PNKFLMGO
PORQPINE	3DOGSRWE
COWS R US	REDNECK1
MOOOO	ELVIS - 10

At least we're friendly!

YOO-HOO	U CAN II
HOWDOUDO	METOO, U2
HOWRUALL	NJOYNJOY
SMYL PAL	2UBPEACE
U B HAPPY	PEACE 2U

CUTE & CLEVER LICENSE PLATES

Those medical people.........lawyers..........realtors

TOP GYN	BABYKCHR	I OBJECT	REALIST8
2PCME	SURGPATH	AT WILL	CME4RST
NURSPWR	CADUCEUS	SOLEPRAC	HOMES4U
PET RN	LUNG DOC	LAWRDOG	ASKARLTR
LTL1SNRS	2THFXR	RES IPSA	DEED 4 U

Those cooks.....aviators..........stockbrokers.....bankers?

LUV2COOK	LV 2 AV8	THE NAZZ	WEALTH4U
COOKIMAN	KPTN SKY	STOXBONZ	BANK$ERV
IAMZCHEF	I AVI8TE	MKTFOCUS	MS. BANK

Other Charlotteans' occupations

INSHRNCE	ARC·TECH	SPKR MAN	BONDSRUS
LFE&HLTH	DIRTKING	SPCH FXR	MULCHER
PAPARA-Z	MUD&ROX	IMAKULAF	BUILDERZ
DEZYNER	REVGRAMA	IDOYRTRV	'HUMBLDR2
COURTRPR	DNTREMVR	IKUTHAIR	IBUILDM2
BRAKEGUY	DENT DR	ILUVTCHN	EDUK8R
STORYGUY	IRON DOC	1TO1MKTR	M'BALM'R

CUTE & CLEVER LICENSE PLATES

ArtSpeak........	SongSpeak.......	MusicSpeak......	DanceSpeak
VP 4 ART	SINGSING	FRETBURN	DANCFRK1
MINT2BE	DUETNE1?	MUSIKMKR	SHAGGING
ITZ ART	SUEPRANO	MUSICMXR	STARDNCR
DA ARTS	SINGALOT	TUBACZAR	WEIRDNCN'
"DRAWS"	CANTICLE	IN2SAXES	22 TANGO

Procrastinators

		Control freaks?	
L84WRK	RUNNLATE	SLOWDOWN	SMOKEONE
L84DINR	ONOIML8	BUK L UP	UDOTHAT
L8FAMILY	ONOL8AGN	NOEXQCES	U R FIRED
L8ICUOFN	THDOG8IT	GETEM'ON	TTLCNTRL

Someone's bragging bigtime!

		Wishful thinkers!	
MAVEN	SAVED 24	#1SONWES	IWANTPAR
GLDINLAY	GR8RUN	#ONEBRAT	2FEWPARS
WEPRO$PR	ZUMBYU	XWIZIT	#1 T TIME
2ME 4ME	CMEONTV?	HELUVSME	IKNOTHAT
ONLY1ME	2HOLESN1	B LIKE ME	GWBUSH
GLAMOUR	7XCHAMPN	PWRESUME	4EVRYUNG
FANCNANC	2BZTOP	UWANTHIS	SEEKN'HB!

CUTE & CLEVER LICENSE PLATES

Definitely female!

CHARGEIT	BABYDOL	BBY BOO
DDYLGIRL	BLONNDEE	PRINCESS
DEDZGIRL	SWT BABY	FOXXXY

Definitely male!

UMMBABY!	BLT4UTUF	BABES!
BIGGIRAT	TOY-4-RAY	WLD BILL
I'M A FOX	OUTFOX	DAWGHSE2

Creatively clever?

EWENSEA	ST8ISGR8	NEES NU2
YOOVEAY	H2OXRCIZ	10-ANT
4YOUNC	SAVR4EST	4TUNE8
DEAC N S	LIFS2SRT	CRE8IVE1

Or just a poor speller?

PNCLPSHR	RKNCILD	MINDBNDR
BLUBYEWE	BIPSYCLE	MIND/MTR
CZYRDREM	KRPEDIEM	NRGIZER
RCEU2TOP	KARPEDIM	LYSDEXIC

Makes you wonder, huh?

WOOZIE	THE GNAT!	IMINXTCY
SNOOZEN	DUNTHAT2	X TA CY
MYRX&ME	MZBHAVEN	THUG-LUV
WILDWMN	GRIPNRIP	NTGUILTY
SQRL2MOM	BARBER-Q	PROBE'IN
PHATLADY	SCANDALL	XNTRIC 1
OBCMAN	BREATH	XIMA
FAT BEAR	SWORDMAN	SHYLOCK

Worry, too!......Oh, boy!

CR8HAVOK	BEAMMIUP	PSY CHIC
TRMAJNKY	UCAUFO	"NUTT"
GOOFYONE	LASTJEDI	HYPNOS
BATTYONE	UZ TH 4CE	VAMPYRE
BATTI 2	NRVUSREK	CRASH
INTHRAPY	SHOOTIST	ST8EDGE
FIND'NME	MABARKER	ICTHRUU
DNG-A-LNG	WYBNRML	TOTLKAOS

CUTE & CLEVER LICENSE PLATES

They're wondering, too!

GOTANY?S   DO IOU 2?
WHATZNU?   WHR2NOW?
82BRUTE?   RUKDNME
JUSTW8&C   Y KNOT
5X=#*?   2B-NOT2B

Sports car/luxury/ convertible breed:

KWIK CAR (red)
MI PLACE (red)
RDROCKET (red)
COPMAGNT (red))
INS-2-HI! (Corvette)
2CTR14U (convertible)
IDSRVIT (luxury)
INDULGED (Jaguar)
JEALOUS? (Lexus)
POOR (Lexus)
WAS HIS (black sports car; blonde "honey")

Wishing to be somewhere else?

JAW JUH   LV$NV
GNUYAWKA   LUVTHMTN
NY-A-DUDE   OCNILBCH
NOTRHOME   WLDAKKRS
GR82B4ND   MAINEAC

Other Charlotte Curiosities:

A BASIN (looks like a BMW to me!)
PORSCHE 1 (on a Jaguar)
1UGLYSUV (odd-colored Jeep)
YOMOMA (stationwagon driven by "cool" middle-aged mom)
YES MAM! (Same mama. New luxury car. No teenagers.)
THEGIRL'S (guy driving)
SLICKS DAD (woman driving)
SEATBELT (in plastic surgeons' parking lot)
THE BRIDE (white VW & bouquet on dash)
LUVU.COM (couple met on internet)
BOTLNECK (a true Charlottean!)

CUTE & CLEVER BUSINESS NAMES

Charlotte business owners have outdone themselves thinking up clever (okay, sometimes cock-eyed cuckoo) names. Just for fun, cover the plain text while reading the list in bold print and try to guess the category. Don't believe us? Check the Yellow Pages ©.

A Bare Affair	strip-o-grams	**All Out**	chimney sweep
A Clear Choice	window cleaning	**Always Smile**	teeth whitening ctrs.
A Closet Full	women's apparel	**Ark**	movers
A Dog's Best Friend	pet grooming	**Art Attack**	graphic designers
A Heaven Scent	florist	**Artful Dodger**	art gallery/framing
A Pal's Best Pals	pet sitting	**Artistcape**	lawn maintenance
A Sign of the Times	special occ. signs	**At My Wit's End**	billiard center
A Sweet Affair	bakers	**Auto Verks**	Mercedes auto shop
About Face	hair removing	**Bag It Up**	handbags
Add In's & Add On's	home improvements	**Beck & Call**	concierge services
Adjustments Made	home improvements	**Bedside Manor**	bedding
Affairs to Remember	caterers	**Big Dipper**	ice cream store
Aging Beauty	home hair stylists	**Blast Master**	sandblasting
Alien Ink	tattooing	**Body by Design**	personal training

CUTE & CLEVER BUSINESS NAMES

Branching Out	nursery
Brideshead	bridal headpieces
Brilliant Deductions	tax return preparers
Bug-Out	pest control
Cat Hat	novelties
Charlotte Live	nightclub
Choose to be Free	fitness programs
Claws & Paws	pet grooming
Clean Can	portable toilets
Clean Solutions	janitorial service
Clearly Superior	windshield repair
Clothes Horse	women's apparel
Color Coat	painters
Copy Cat	printers
Cradle & All	interiors-baby rooms
Dan the Man/Bob the Cat	concrete contractor
Down to Earth	lawn care
Dust Bunnies	house cleaning
ESP Supply Center	occult supplies
Finders R Us	private investigators
Fintastic	tropical fish store
First In Counters	counter tops
Flag to Flag	racing scanners
Flying Saucers	pottery
For Pets' Sake	pet sitting
Fringe Benefits	custom draperies
Get the Lead Out	environmental cnslt.
Go Getters	movers
Go Home	real estate
Gofors	delivery service
Great Stuff	old & new gifts
Groomingdales	pet grooming
Grout Surgeons	ceramic tile repairs
Gym Dandies	gymnastics
Head to Tail	pet shop
Heroes Aren't Hard to Find	old comics/hobbies
Home Surgeons	cosmetic srgy-home
Honeychile	Southern gifts
Hot Shots	modeling/photog.
House of Threads	bolts & nuts
Ice House	skating rink
Immortal Images	tattooing

CUTE & CLEVER BUSINESS NAMES

Jollyair	heating contractors
K-9 Cleaners	pet grooming
Karat Patch	jewelers
Killo	Killough's pest cntrl
Kneaded Touch	massage therapist
Knit Wits	needlework store
Last Call	private club
Last Pitcher Show	bar
Last Place on Earth	pet shop
Let's Go Outside	nursery (plants)
Mad Dash	errand service
Maid in Heaven	house cleaning
Mindboggle	video arcade
Mind Your Own Business	office management
More Than Manners	business consultants
Morning Dew	landscape irrigation
Moving Poets	dance theater
Nerds 4 Rent	computer service
Nip Drip	handyman-plumbing
On Track	modeling agency
One of a Find	consignment shop
Out to Lunch	caterers
Over Stock Market	gift shop
Pair-A-Dice	travel agency
Pawsitively Pampered	pet sitting
Peachy Clean	house cleaning
Perfect Paws	pet grooming
Pillar to Post	home inspections
Posh Pets	pet-o-tel
Principal First	financing
Quiche & Tell	caterers
Quick Fix	jewelry repairs
Regyp	Sheetrock recycling
Rock It Tops	cabinet tops
Rock,Paper,Scissors	invitations
Run for Your Life	sporting goods
Run-In	convenience store
Sign Up	sign company
Sky's the Limit	commercial photog.
Soap Box	coin laundry
Special K Enrichment	day care
Squeaky Clean	house cleaning
Stress Arrest	day spa

CUTE & CLEVER BUSINESS NAMES

Super Duper	grocer
Sweet Charlotte	gourmet desserts
Sweet Repeats	consignment shop
Taj Mahall	nightclub
Talk 'N Trash	rubbish removal
That Other Place	beauty salon
The Bag Lady	women's stuff
The Blind Doctor	window blinds
The Bodhi Tree	yoga instruction
The Playroom	music instruction
The Right Gear	bicycle shop
The Write Design	graphic designers
Total Xperience	nightclub
Twin Peeks	nightclub
Under One Roof	roofing contractors
Unfauxgettable	murals
Wax Museum	used records, tapes
Weir Dancin'	dance studio
Window Dresser	window blinds
Woof & Hoof	horse supplies
Yachta, Yachta Yachta	charters

HUH?

Armored Dragon	graphic designer
Brown Bag Studio	bldg. restoration
Chocolate Soup	kids' clothes
Crazy Jane's	home furnishings
Dragon Dreams	limo service
Freddy's Armadillo	nightclub
Fresh Produce	skateboard shop
Golden Goose	kids clothes
I. C. London	lingerie
Lavender-N-Lace	pet shop
Peaceful Dragon	martial arts
Pink Fairy	travel agents
PuddleDucks	ice cream factory
Pure Body	hair stylists
Seed	handmade gifts
Steel Moon	funky gifts
The 8th Wonder	home & gift items
Upside Down Turtle	waste rags & crafts
Very Chihuahua	jewelry
What's Happening	carpets

CUTE & CLEVER BUSINESS NAMES

Beauty salon owners have the most imaginative shop names. Here are some of our favorites and a few musings and ponderings:

Adam & Eve (Beware of the sssssnake!), **Ain't It Great Limited** (If it's so great, why is it limited?), **Anointed Touch** (Anointed by whom and with what?), **Audacious** (Reckless & insolent?), **Bang Bang** (As in forehead hair or you're dead?), **Beehive** ('60s bzzz!), **Changing Faces** (Wrong side of the head!), **Compliment's** (Proprietor's name?), **Curl's** (Surely, this is not the owner's name! Or is it?) **and Swirls, Cut 'N Up** (Oh, oh, look out!), **The Green Iguana** (Say what?), **Hair Factory** (An assembly line?), **Hair I Am** (Must be itchy!), **Hair It Is** (Thair it goes!), **Hair Razors** (A real scary idea!), **Hair's the Limit** (Why one hair?), **Hair X-Scape** (Where?), **Hair-y Care-y** (Sportscaster or ritual suicide?), **I Kut Hair & Kompany** (I don't want to be company!), **The Ladies Room** (How many potties?), **Lap of Luxury** (Lap? Isn't that the wrong end?), **Looks Familiar** (I hope so.), **Miracles** (For the really desperate.), **Mirage** (An illusion for boyfriends in a fog.), **More Than Conqueror** (With swords or cannons?), **NuDu** (Old "dos" would never do.), **Obsessions** (When your hair rules your life.), **Planet 21** (For outer space appearances?), **Purrfection** (For kitties?), **Scarlett O'Haira's** (Will he give a damn?), **Secrets** (Only your hairdresser knows for sure.), **Snobbs** (By or for?), **Straight Mary** (Won't touch that one!), **Tangles** (Don't tangles hurt?), **Three Blondes Salon** (So why seven phone numbers?), **Top Shop** (Please, no bottoms.), **Wave Lengths** (Are they on yours?), **What Nails You** (Hammers!), **Who's That Lady** (We give up.), **You Too** (Thanks! You, too.) and our favorite: **Another Bad Creation** (Enough said.).

LOCAL SPORTS HISTORY QUIZ

Try This!

Think you know a lot about sports? Here's a local sports history trivia quiz, a challenge from homegrown fan, Jack Wood. Think way, way back!

GENERAL SPORTS

1. When was the American Legion Memorial Stadium completed and what was its opening event?

2. What had been on that stadium's site previously?

3. When was the "old" coliseum (now the Independence Arena) built and what was its opening event?

4. Which school had the only gymnasium in the county in 1926?

5. What was Charlotte's oldest continuous sports event?

6. Name the second oldest continuous sports event.

LOCAL SPORTS HISTORY QUIZ

7. Name two Charlotteans who have won the Sullivan Award (best amateur athletes).

8. What did Otto Gullickson pioneer?

9. What Charlottean was a star in four sports at UNC in the 1920s?

10. Who was "Hard Rock" Simpson and what did he do at Griffith Park?

11. What high school coach's teams won 3 football, 4 basketball and 2 baseball championships from 1929 to 1934?

12. Where and when was the NC Sports Hall of Fame founded? Where is it now?

13. Name the first 5 inductees in the NC Sports Hall of Fame.

14. What was the city's first international sports event. Where was it held?

BASEBALL

1. What Charlottean sponsored the first Carolina League team in 1902?

2. What was the Twilight League?

3. Who were the team owners of the 1920's Charlotte pro baseball team and where did they play their home games?

LOCAL SPORTS HISTORY QUIZ

4. Who was Charlotte's first major league player?

5. Name the 18-year-old local player who, during his first game as a New York Giant, hit a home run his first time at bat.

6. What former Charlotte Hornet first baseman won the American League batting title in 1932?

7. Name some of the players on Cal Griffith's Charlotte Hornets team who later were regulars in the major leagues.

8. Who is the pitcher from Mecklenburg County who holds several major league records and is in the Baseball Hall of Fame?

9. Name the Charlotte player who was a Yankee with "Babe" Ruth, Lou Gehrig, Bill Dickey, Bob Muesel, Joe Dugan and Tony Lazzeri.

10. The Hornets at Griffith Park were a farm team for which major league team?

FOOTBALL

1. What team was Charlotte's first to win a state high school championship?

2. Name the city's first professional football team and their playing field.

LOCAL SPORTS HISTORY QUIZ

3. Who was the Charlotte player who scored the first two touchdowns in UNC's new Kenan Stadium?

4. Who was Charlotte's "Crooning Halfback"?

5. What major historical event occurred during a Charlotte Clippers game?

6. Who was Davidson's only All-American football player?

7. What Davidson player got in "Ripley's Believe It or Not" and why?

8. Our first college All-American went to what high school and college?

9. Name the All-Pro player from the NFL who went to high school and college in Charlotte. Which local schools did he play for?

10. A Second Ward High player made All-American at Minnesota and played with the Giants for 6 years. Who was he and what position did he play?

11. What was the Queen City Classic?

BASKETBALL

1. What Charlotte businessman played on the original YMCA team in Springfield, MA, when Dr. James Naismith originated basketball in 1891?

2. Who were the McCachren brothers?

LOCAL SPORTS HISTORY QUIZ

3. Where and when was NC's first interracial basketball game played?

4. Who were the Carolina/Charlotte Monograms? Name some players.

5. Who were Davidson's All-American basketball stars?

6. Name UNC-C's All-American basketball player and the pro team he signed with.

7. Who was the first local high school basketball player to make All-American in college?

GOLF

1. Name Charlotte's golf courses in the 1930s.

2. What local golfer won the NC Amateur Tournament in 1932 and played in it 50 years later?

3. Who was Clayton Heafner?

4. Name the players on Central High's team that won the Southern Championship.

5. Where and when was Charlotte's first PGA Tournament? Who won it?

LOCAL SPORTS HISTORY QUIZ

TENNIS
    1. Who was Teddy Burwell?
    2. Who hosted the Mid-Atlantic Tournament in 1937? Name some of the outstanding players.

BOXING
    1. Who was Charlotte's first National Golden Gloves champion?
    2. Where were the earliest boxing matches held in Charlotte?
    3. Two brothers were promoters in the '20s and '30s. Who were they?
    4. What Charlotte boxer fought Joe Louis?
    5. Name some of the outstanding local boxers from the early days.

TRACK & FIELD
    1. What Charlotte/Central High School track coach led his teams to win state titles every year from 1924 to 1931 (except 1928, when he did not coach)?
    2. Name some of the state record-holders from those years.
    3. What record was broken at a '35 Charlotte Jaycees Indoor Track Meet?

LOCAL SPORTS HISTORY QUIZ

4. Which local college athlete held the world 400 meter track record?

5. What Charlotte athlete won Olympic bronze medals in 1948 & 1952? In which track event?

6. Name the Charlottean who held 5 world records in track at one time.

WRESTLING

1. Where were local wrestling matches held during the '20s?

2. Who were two early world champs who wrestled in Charlotte?

3. Name 2 promoters and some of the wrestlers headquartered at the old Armory Auditorium.

MOTORSPORTS

1. Who was Charlotte's first national champion in motorsports?

2. Where was Charlotte's first major speedway and when did it operate?

3. What kind of autos raced there?

4. What kind of tracks did local stock cars race on in the 1930s?

LOCAL SPORTS HISTORY QUIZ

HORSE RACING

　　1. Where did they have local harness racing?

　　2. What race horse stabled and trained in Mecklenburg County won the harness Triple Crown in 1941?

　　3. Who was the owner of this famous horse?

SWIMMING

　　1. Name the city's public swimming pools in 1930.

　　2. Name the public swimming pools in Mecklenburg County in 1930.

　　3. What Charlotte-born athlete won 4 Olympic gold medals in '64?

OTHER SPORTS

　　1. What local athlete won 4 Southern championships in handball singles competition?

　　2. Who from Charlotte was a speed boat champion in the '30s?

LOCAL SPORTS HISTORY QUIZ

ANSWERS & SCORING

To be fair, scoring must be age-appropriate. There are 76 questions.

If you are over 90, you can rate as a **Charlotte Sports Historian** if you can answer 65. Anyone over 80: 55; over 70: 45; over 60: 35; over 50: 25; over 40: 15; over 30: 5. Everyone else: if you get one right - Congratulations!

GENERAL SPORTS

1. Built by the WPA, it was completed 1936. Opening event: Dedication by President Franklin D. Roosevelt in a Green Pastures Rally.

2. Previously on that site: an amphitheater. Before that: meadow and creek. Before that: the city's water reservoir.

3. The building with the largest unsupported dome in the world opened on September 11, 1955. After a dedication by Dr. Billy Graham, the Ice Capades began a sold-out run.

4. O'Donoghue at South Tryon and 2nd Street. Some school basketball games were played at the Elk's Club, Hawthorne Lane Methodist Church and the YMCA on Tryon Street.

5. Carolinas Golden Gloves, founded in 1933 by Jake Wade and M.H. Brandon. Charlotte residents "Duck" Diehl and Fred Hood were among the participants that first year.

LOCAL SPORTS HISTORY QUIZ

6. Shrine Bowl (football) Game, founded in 1937 by Bob Allen. First year local players: Frank Owens and Tom Smith; first year assistant coach: Jim Morgan.

7. Jim Beatty - track - 1962; Don Schollander - swimming - 1964

8. Physical education in the public schools in the mid-'20s, as the city's first "p.e." director.

9. "Monk" (Dr. Angus) McDonald won 16 monograms at UNC.

10. No baseball player, this postman from Burlington ran around Griffith Park during a 9-inning game. His real claim to fame was running in C.C. Pyle's cross-country "Bunion Derby" and racing a horse and rider until the horse dropped.

11. Walter Skidmore, Central - Football:'29,'30,'32 Basketball:'31-'34 Baseball: '30,'32

12. In Charlotte, 1962. It is now in Raleigh.

13. On April 15, 1963 in Charlotte. Jim Beatty, Wes Ferrell, Charlie Justice, Estelle Lawson Page and Ace Parker were inducted.

14. The Davis Cup zone match: USA vs. Ecuador was held in the old coliseum in 1968. The Davis Cup finals: USA vs. Romania was played at Olde Providence Racquet Club in 1971

BASEBALL

1. F. H. Wearn

2. Teams sponsored by companies in the '20s and '30s. They played in twilight hours.

3. The Hornets, owned by Bud Moore and Felix Hayman, played at Wearn Field at South Mint and West Bland Streets.

4. George Murray, pitcher, Red Sox (college: NC State)

LOCAL SPORTS HISTORY QUIZ

5. "Whitey" Lockman from Paw Creek

6. With a .367 average, Dale Alexander of Detroit and Boston (He was traded mid-season.)

7. Bobby Estelella, Bob Ortiz, Gil Torres, Jake Early, Al Evans, Jimmy Bloodworth, Bucky Jacobs, Joe Haynes, Early Wynn, Ellis Clary

8. Hoyt Wilhelm of Huntersville. Most games pitched: 1070; most relief wins: 123; most saves: 227. Wilhelm played 319 consecutive games without an error.

9. Ben Paschal

10. The Washington Senators, owned by Clark Griffith, who sent his adopted son, Cal Griffith to run the farm team. Cal chose the abandoned name, Hornets, for the local team.

FOOTBALL

1. Charlotte High School, coached by Marvin Ritch, in 1916

2. The Charlotte Bantams (American League) played 1932-34 at Wearn Field. Some of the players were: Johnny Branch, George Houston, Ed McIntosh, "Poss" Kessler, Ray Farris, Harry Schwartz, Ralph Shoup, Bud Shuler, Roy McDade, Ed Williams, Earl Clary, Earl Dunlap, "Bo" Dotherow, Buster Mott, Roy Hoffstetler.

3. Edison Foard, 1927

4. Duke's Nick Laney had his own band before Johnny Long or Les Brown.

5. During a game with Norfolk in Charlotte's Memorial Stadium, the PA announcer told 10,000 fans that the Japs had bombed Pearl Harbor. December 7, 1941.

6. Johnny Mackorell, 1934.

LOCAL SPORTS HISTORY QUIZ

7. Thad Brock went back to punt behind his goal line and ran 103 yards, but didn't score. He was tackled on the 2 yard line.

8. "Pug" Peerman from Harding High went to the University of Tennessee.

9. Pettis Norman -Dallas Cowboys-played for West Charlotte High and Johnson C. Smith.

10. Bill Staton, interior lineman

11. Annual game between the Second Ward Tigers and West Charlotte Lions.

BASKETBALL

1. F.C. Abbot, a realtor.

2. Family basketball team that won a national championship. John was assistant physical director at Charlotte's YMCA. Dave, Jim, Bill and George were all elected captains of their respective basketball teams at UNC.

3. A YMCA team played Johnson C. Smith in December 1936 at the J.C. Smith gym.

4. A semi-pro team in Charlotte. All had earned monograms at UNC. They played barnstorm opponents or "all comers" 1928-1933. Among the players: Artie Newcombe, Sam McDonald, John Purser, Bill Dodderer, Billy Harwell, Carr Purser.

5. Fred Hetzel -'64,'65; Dick Snyder - '66; Mike Maloy - '69,'70

6. Cedric Maxwell ('76,'77) was signed by Boston.

7. Bobby Jones from South Meck made All-American in '74 at UNC, then played for Philadelphia in the NBA.

LOCAL SPORTS HISTORY QUIZ

GOLF
    1. Charlotte Country Club (1st in 1910) - Mecklenburg Avenue, Myers Park Country Club - Roswell Avenue, McClintock - Central Avenue, Mammoth Oaks- off Providence Road, Carolina - Old Steele Creek Road and Revolution Park, the city's municipal course
    2. Erwin Laxton
    3. Local club pro who was runner-up to Ben Hogan in the U.S. Open in 1951
    4. Erwin Laxton, Fred McCanless, Bayard Storm, Irvin Boyle
    5. The Charlotte Open at Myers Park Country Club in 1944 was won by Dutch Harrison (in uniform). In 1945, Byron Nelson won. The last Charlotte Open was in 1948.

TENNIS
    1. Charlottean who made the Davis Cup team in the early '30s as an alternate. He lost a close march to Rene LaCoste in the quarter-finals at Wimbledon.
    2. Myers Park Country Club. Outstanding players: (national) Bill Tilden, Bitsy Grant; (local) Teddy Burwell, Bob Crosland, Bo Roddey, Julia Pickens (later Southern champ).

BOXING
    1. Clifford Smith (1943)
    2. The old auditorium on North College at East 5th. Later: Charlotte Armory, jail yard on South Mint Street, and Memorial Stadium.
    3. Al and Sol Tenner

LOCAL SPORTS HISTORY QUIZ

4. Leo Johnson in an exhibition match

5. Lukie Tenner, Crayton Rowe, Ralph Hood, Dave Edelman. Later: Jimmy Swinson, Lou Kemp, Rufus Miles.

TRACK & FIELD

1. Dr. Harvey Barrett

2. Phil Gallagher, Wade Ison, Dave Neiman, John Fort, Guy Soule, Oscar Mullis, Harold Sutton, Tom Hawthorne

3. Jack Torrence of LSU set the world mark in indoor shot put

4. Vince Matthews of Johnson C. Smith

5. Floyd ("Chunk") Simmons - the Decathlon

6. Jim Beatty broke the 4-minute indoor mile (3:58.9) February 10, 1962. He also held the records for the indoor 2 miles, outdoor 2 miles, indoor 1500 meters, indoor 2,000 meters.

WRESTLING

1. The old auditorium on North College

2. Wladek Zbysko and Ed ("Strangler") Lewis

3. Promoters: Irish Horan and Jim Crockett Wrestlers: Jim Henry, Joe Savoldi, Mayes McLain, "Cowboy" Luttrell, Herman Hickman

LOCAL SPORTS HISTORY QUIZ

MOTORSPORTS
    1. Doug Creech, motorcyclist in '20s & '30s (next: "Buck" Brigance)
    2. The board track with wooden stands (on Pineville Road near where Lance is now) opened October 24, 1924. The last race there was in October 1927.
    3. Indianapolis race cars
    4. Dirt tracks like the one near the Fairgrounds off Tuckaseegee Road

HORSE RACING
    1. Near the Fairgrounds off Tuckaseegee Road
    2. The Trotter, Bill Gallon. Triple Crown: Futurity, Thompson Memorial, Hambletonian
    3. Horace Johnston

SWIMMING
    1. None
    2. Mammoth Oaks off Providence, Wilora Lake off Lawyers Road, Sustar's in Matthews and McAlpine's on Monroe Road
    3. Don Schollander - 100 meters, 400 meters and 2 team relays

OTHER SPORTS
    1. Eddie Sloan at Knoxville '38, Charleston '39, Richmond '47, Knoxville '49
    2. Doug Creech (yep, the national motorcycle champion)

Other Humor Titles by A. Borough Books
If you enjoyed this book, you're sure to like:

You Can Tell You're a Charlottean If...
288 ways that residents (natives, newcomers and long-timers) of Charlotte, NC are different from the rest of the world + Head Scratchers & Queenz Quiz. 91 locals contributed lines.
Margaret Bigger & Betsy Webb Cartoons by Loyd Dillon
LARGE PRINT - 1998   Paperback   pp. 96 $7.95

MEN! Cry Flustered Frustrated Females Everywhere
True MALE TALES, GIVENS & HOW COMES from 44 of those FFFs proving that typical men don't think/act/talk like typical females. Margaret G. Bigger Cartoons by Loyd Dillon
LARGE PRINT - 2000   Paperback   pp. 96 $7.50

Churchgoers' Chuckles
True Tales - You Can't Make This Stuff Up! Anecdotes from 97 churchgoers in 16 denominations and 30 states. Margaret G. Bigger Cartoons by Loyd Dillon
LARGE PRINT - 2000   Paperback   pp. 96 $7.50

Kitties & All That Litter
Mewsings, GRRRoaners, true cat tales and kitty limericks by 26 cat-loving curmudgeons.
Edited/Curtailed by Margaret G. Bigger Cat-tooned by Loyd Dillon
LARGE PRINT - 1999   Paperback   pp. 96 $7.50

You've GOT to Have a Sense of Humor to Have a Wedding

Humorous, outrageous & disastrous true tales from the engagement through the honeymoon + advice not found in wedding guides.   Margaret G. Bigger   Cartoons by Loyd Dillon
Standard print - 1997, Third Printing April 1998   Paperback pp. 128 $9.95

MotherHoot - The Lighter Side of Motherhood

True anecdotes about moms from pregnancy through grandmotherhood + MotherHoot Tips for
 sanity   Margaret G. Bigger   Cartoons by Loyd Dillon
Standard print - 1999, Second Printing June 1999   Paperback pp. 128 $9.95

Gray-Haired Grins & Giggles

Guess What! Grammy & Grandy have a sense of humor, too! True tales from childhood to
 retirement by 45 senior authors Margaret G. Bigger Cartoons by Loyd Dillon
Standard print - 1995, Fourth Printing June 1996 Paperback   pp. 128 $12.95
LARGE PRINT - 1998, somewhat abridged   Paperback   pp. 140 $13.95

See order form - next page.

What's Next?
DaddyHoot - The Lighter Side of Fatherhood
Puppies & All That Waggin'
Kitties & All That Litter, Vol. II.
MEN! WOMEN!
Churchgoers' Chuckles, Vol. II
ParentHoot - The Lighter Side of Parenthood

Order Form

Please complete both sides of this form.

_____ copies of **You Know You're In Charlotte If...**

At the retail price of $7.95 $_____

_____copies of _____(other title)

At the retail price of _____ $_____

Plus $2 postage/handling up to 5 books; $4 up to 10 books $_____

NC residents add 6.5% state tax on retail price to:
                                    TOTAL $_____

Autographed? Yes_____ No_____

If you want your books autographed,
     please give this information so that the book can be personalized as a gift.

In Charlotte or Charlottean book to_____

Reason recipient would like it _____

Men book to _____Name of her man_____

Chuckles book to_____His/her church_____

Wedding book to_____Wedding date_____
  Circle: Bride &/or groom Mother of the bride Minister/priest/rabbi

Motherhood book to:_____ Kids' names_____
        Circle: Expectant mom   Mother   Grandmother

Cat book to:_____Cats' names_____

Senior humor book to:_____

Your name/ address/ phone number:

Mail form & check to: **A. Borough Books, P.O. Box 15391 Charlotte, NC 28211**